This book is lovingly presented to

_____

For My Grandchild

An album of memories from grandparent to grandchild

Pictures by
Karen Maloof

Ideals Publishing Corporation • Nashville, Tennessee

Published by Ideals Publishing Corporation
Nashville, Tennessee 37210

Printed and bound in the United States of America.

ISBN 0-8249-8545-1

For Mom

Special thanks to:
Larry Buksbaum, Mr. and Mrs. Gabe Hakim, Planting Fields
Arboretum, Vic and Chris Samra, Lauren Brunhofer, and
Glen Maloof.   – K.M.

The display type was set in LeGriffe and Berkeley Bold.
The text type was set in Berkeley Book.
Color separations were made by Web Tech, Inc.,
Butler, Wisconsin.
Printed and bound by Worzalla Publishing,
Stevens Point, Wisconsin.

Designed by Stacy Venturi-Pickett.

This volume is designed to help you provide your grandchild with a personal, lasting record of the lives of those held dear. This family heirloom features ample space for recording the dates, names, and places of importance and, even more significantly, room for sharing the impressions, feelings, and hopes of your lifetime.

The text pages of For My Grandchild *offer oversized areas for records, which let you choose the most important details without requiring their inclusion. And exquisitely designed borders showcase family photographs which you will share with your grandchild.*

Complemented by beautiful hand-tinted images of home and family, each entry and every moment recorded renders immortal the memories of lifetimes, straight to the heart of your grandchild from your own loving hand.

Our family tree

Grandchild

Mother

Father

Grandmother

Grandfather

Grandmother

Grandfather

Great-Grandmother

Great-Grandmother

Great-Grandmother

Great-Grandmother

Great-Grandfather

Great-Grandfather

Great-Grandfather

Great-Grandfather

About Great-Grandmother

Birth of Great-Grandmother

    date

    place

Parents

Brothers and sisters

Hometown

Education

Wedding

    date

    place

Career

Personality

About Great-Grandmother

Birth of Great-Grandmother

date

place

Parents

Brothers and sisters

Hometown

Education

Wedding

date

place

Career

Personality

Great-Grandmothers' stories

About Great-Grandfather

Birth of Great-Grandfather

    date

    place

Parents

Brothers and sisters

Hometown

Education

Military service

Career

Personality

Birth of Great-Grandfather

    date

    place

Parents

Brothers and sisters

Hometown

Education

Military service

Career

Personality

Great-Grandfathers' stories

About Grandmother

Birth of Grandmother

    date

    place

Hair color

Eye color

Complexion

Family resemblances

Brothers and sisters

Story behind name

Personality

About Grandfather

Birth of Grandfather

date

place

Hair color

Eye color

Complexion

Family resemblances

Brothers and sisters

Story behind name

Personality

Photo space

Grandmother's early memories

Hometown

House

Bedroom

Pets

School

After-school activities

Childhood ambitions

Grandfather's early memories

Hometown

House

Bedroom

Pets

School

After-school activities

Childhood ambitions

Grandmother's childhood days

Photo space

Grandfather's childhood days

Grandparents' childhood favorites

Toys and games

Stories

School subjects

Friends

Vacations

Mischief

Foods

Grandmother's young adulthood

Graduation

Ambitions

First occupation

Hobbies

Recreation

Grandfather's young adulthood

Graduation

Ambitions

First occupation

Hobbies

Recreation

About Grandparents' days

World news

Local news

Prominent people

Clothing styles

Current prices

Slang expressions

Popular entertainers

Popular music

Craziest fad

A typical date

Grandparents' courtship

First met

Impressions

Courtship

Proposal

Engagement

Grandparents' wedding

Wedding date and place

Number of attendants and guests

Bridal gown

Groom's suit

Favorite memory

Funniest event

Reception

Honeymoon

Photo space

Grandparents' early wedded years

Hometown

First house

Home decor

Grandmother's work

Grandfather's work

Hobbies

Favorite entertainment

Our relationship

First learned your parent was expected

Birth of

    date

    place

Height

Weight

Hair color

Eye color

Complexion

Family resemblances

Brothers and sisters

Story behind name

Personality

Your parent's early childhood

Hometown

House

Bedroom

Pets

School

After-school activities

Childhood ambitions

Photo space

Favorite memories of parent as child

Your parent's childhood days

Relationships with siblings

Proudest moment

Biggest punishment

Funniest moment

Personality

Special traits

Your parent as a teenager

First occupation

Recreation

Craziest fad your parent engaged in

Parent rebelled when

Proudest moment

Photo space

Your parents' courtship and wedding

First met

Impressions

Engagement

Wedding date and place

Number of attendants and guests

Bridal gown

Groom's suit

Favorite memory

Funniest event

Reception

Honeymoon

Photo space

Dear Grandchild

First learned you were expected

Birth of

    date

    place

Height

Weight

Hair color

Eye color

Complexion

Family resemblances

Brothers and sisters

Story behind name

Personality

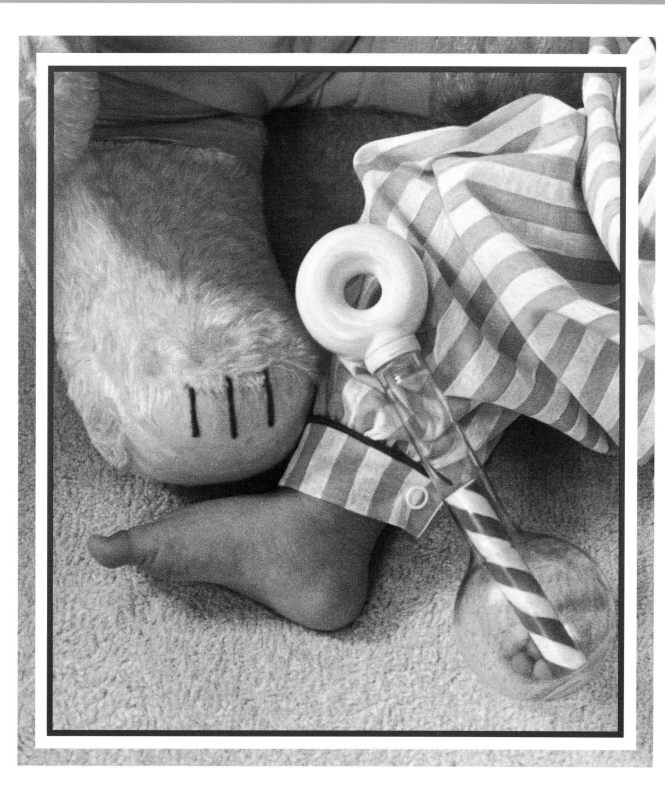

Your childhood days

Relationships with siblings

Proudest moment

Biggest punishment

Funniest moment

Personality

Special traits

Photo space

Photo space

Other stories for you

My wish for you in life